To my precious children,
who make every page of my life worth writing.

Copyright © 2024 Allyson Blindert

All rights reserved. No part of this publication may be reproduced, stored in a retrieval system, or transmitted, in any form or by any means, electronic, mechanical, photocopying, recording, or otherwise, without the prior written permission of the copyright owner.

ISBN: 979-8-9894508-5-5

allysonblindert.com

Slow To Anger

"THE LORD IS MERCIFUL AND COMPASSIONATE, SLOW TO GET ANGRY AND FILLED WITH UNFAILING LOVE."
PSALMS 145:8

IS THERE A TIME THAT YOU CAN REMEMBER FEELING...

ANGRY?

WHAT MADE YOU FEEL LIKE THAT?

HOW DID YOU HANDLE IT?

DID YOU EXPLODE
YOUR FEELINGS

LIKE AN
OVER FULL
BALLOON?

LIFE CAN BE TOUGH SOMETIMES!

WE ARE HUMAN, AND WE HAVE HUMAN FEELINGS.

WE CAN HAVE SO

MANY DIFFERENT FEELINGS!

LET'S BE
SILLY
TOGETHER!

OGABALOOOOO!
OOOOOOGA!
WONKU WILLA!
POMPADOOOODLE!

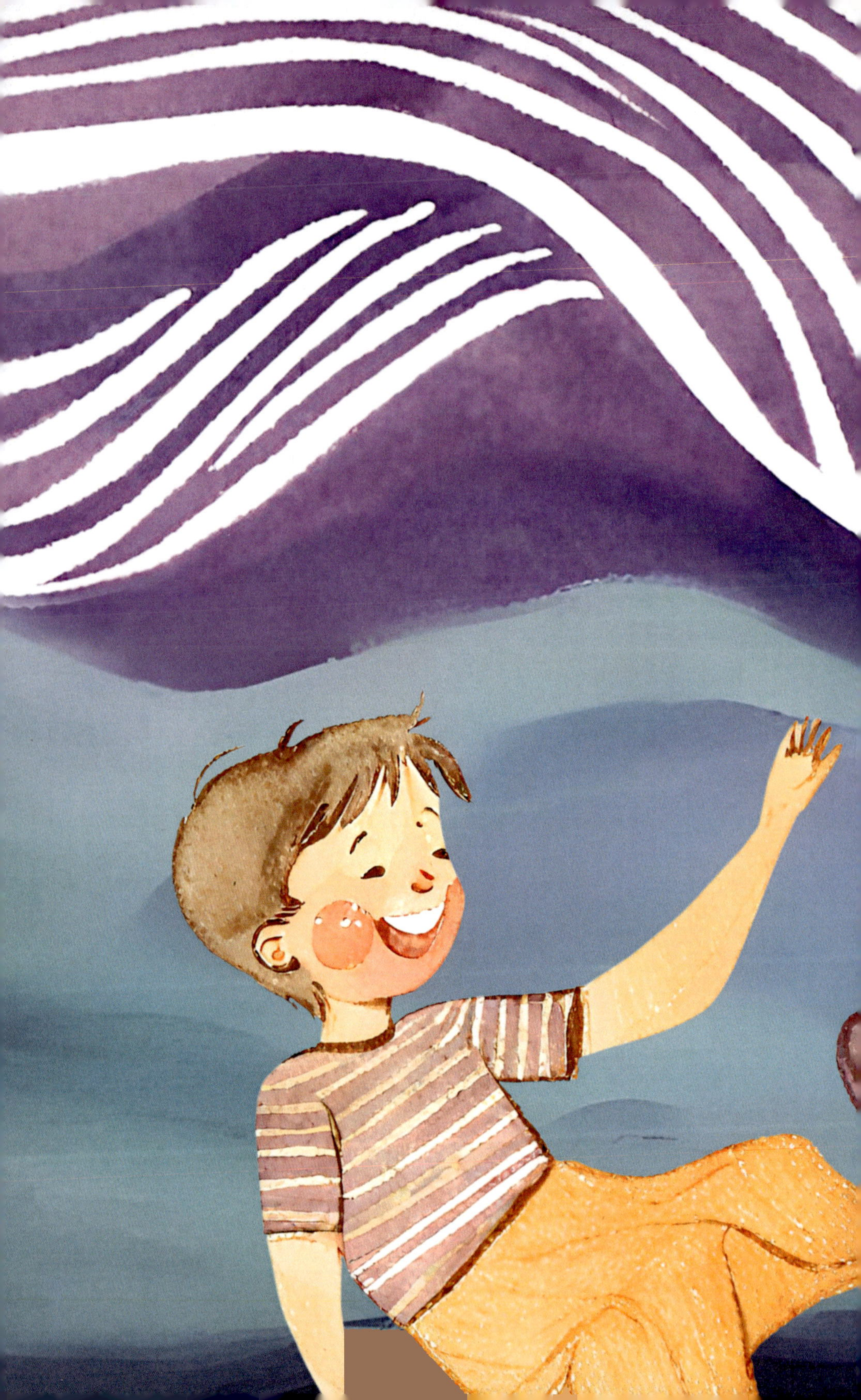

IT'S FUN TO
BE SILLY!

SOMETIMES
WE CAN FEEL...
ANGRY!

HAVE YOU EVER STOMPED YOUR FOOT LIKE...

AN ELEPHANT?

MAYBE YOU DIDN'T
GET WHAT YOU WANTED
RIGHT WHEN YOU WANTED IT.

OR MAYBE SOMEONE SAID SOMETHING THAT HURT YOUR FEELINGS.

YOUR FEELINGS

MATTER!

WE JUST HAVE TO FIGURE OUT A WAY TO **SLOW DOWN**

AND NOT POP LIKE AN OVER FULL BALLOON!

THE FIRST THING WE SHOULD DO IS

STOP AND PRAY!

PRAY THAT GOD WILL GIVE YOU

PEACE AND PATIENCE

DURING THIS TOUGH TIME.

TALKING TO SOMEONE THAT YOU TRUST CAN ALSO BE VERY HELPFUL.

KEEPING OUR BIG FEELINGS INSIDE CAN MAKE THINGS SO MUCH HARDER.

AS HUMANS...

WE ARE SOMETIMES VERY QUICK TO BECOMING ANGRY...

AREN'T WE?

GOD IS SLOW TO ANGER,

AND WE WANT TO BE MORE LIKE HIM.

THAT MEANS WE WANT TO BE SLOW TO GETTING ANGRY TOO!

AS YOU GROW UP
IT WILL TAKE
PRACTICE TO
LEARN HOW TO
HANDLE...

YOUR FEELINGS AND EMOTIONS.

ALWAYS REMEMBER,

WHAT YOU FEEL INSIDE MATTERS!

IT MATTERS TO GOD.

HE CARES ABOUT EVERYTHING YOU ARE GOING THROUGH.

BIG

AND SMALL

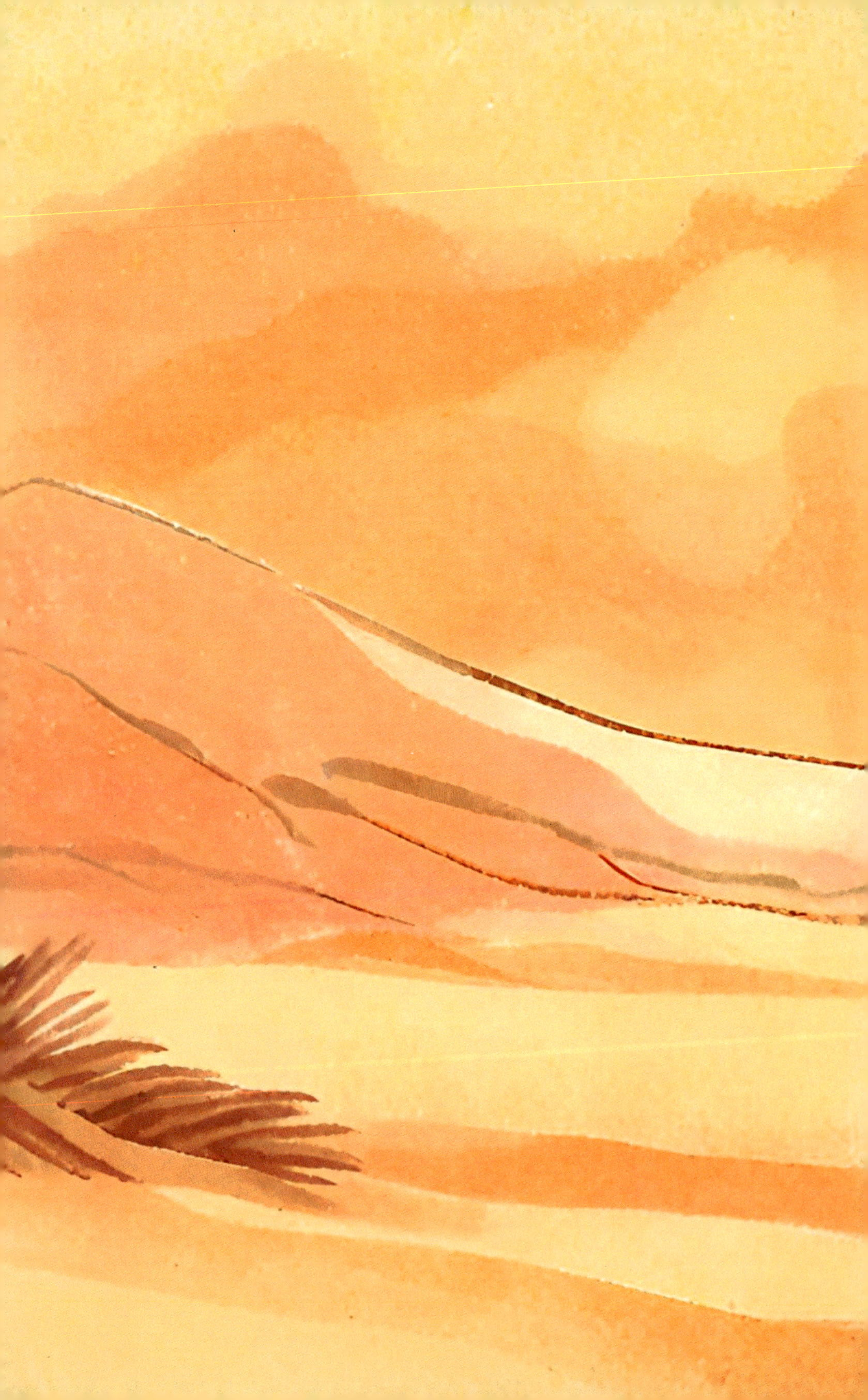

HE IS WAITING TO HELP YOU, ALL YOU HAVE TO DO IS ASK!

IF YOU NEED MORE PATIENCE, **ASK FOR IT!**

IF YOU NEED HELP FIGURING OUT HOW TO NOT POP LIKE AN ANGRY BALLOON,

HE WILL HELP YOU!

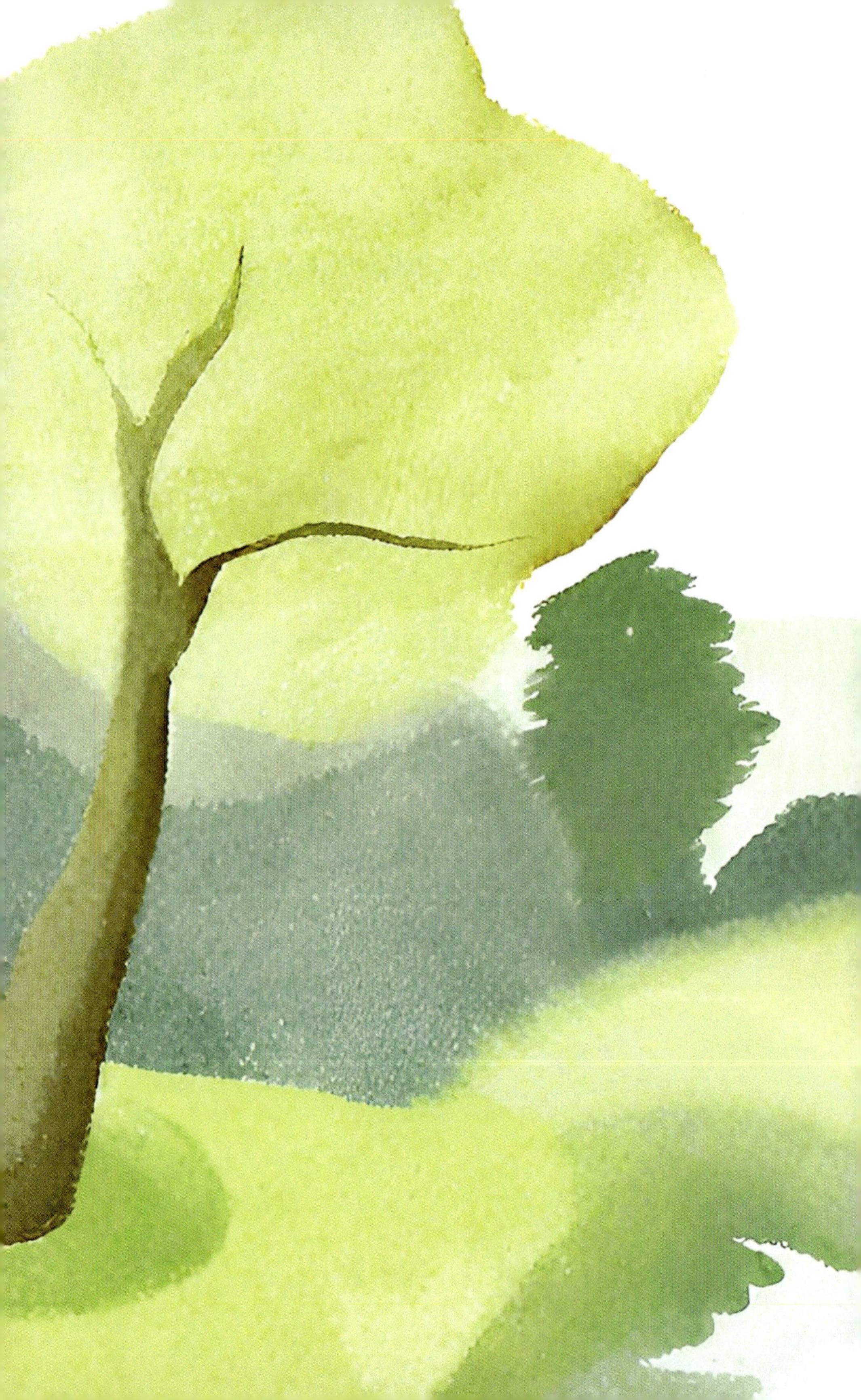

HEY GOD, SOMETIMES I FEEL ANGRY. I DON'T WANT TO FEEL THIS WAY. HELP ME TO BE PATIENT AND LEARN WAYS TO CALM MYSELF. PLEASE TAKE AWAY MY ANGER AND GIVE ME PEACE IN MY HEART! THANK YOU FOR HELPING ME AND LOVING ME!
IN JESUS' NAME I PRAY, AMEN

ENCOURAGING TIP

THE NEXT TIME YOU START TO FEEL ANGRY:

FIND SOMEONE THAT YOU CAN TRUST THAT WILL TALK AND PRAY WITH YOU. STEP AWAY AND FIND SOMETHING TO DO THAT WILL HELP CALM YOU. LISTEN TO MUSIC, DRAW, STRETCH AND BREATHE. SIT QUIETLY AND THINK OF SOMETHING YOU CAN HEAR, SMELL, SEE, AND TOUCH. TRY TO MEMORIZE A BIBLE VERSE ABOUT BEING **SLOW TO ANGER**.

Made in United States
Orlando, FL
27 February 2025